A ROOKIE BIOGRAPHY

ABRAHAM LINCOLN

President of a Divided Country

By Carol Greene

CHILDRENS PRESS®
CHICAGO

This book is for Sara, Mollie, and Kate Edgar.

Abraham Lincoln (1809-1865)

Library of Congress Cataloging-in-Publication Data

Greene, Carol.
    Abraham Lincoln : president of a divided country / by Carol Greene
      p. cm. — (A Rookie biography)
    Includes index.
    Summary: A simple biography of the Civil War president.
    ISBN 0-516-04206-8
    1. Lincoln, Abraham, 1809-1865—Juvenile literature. 2. Presidents—
United States—Biography—Juvenile literature.
[1. Lincoln, Abraham, 1809-1865. 2. Presidents.]
I. Title. II. Series: Greene, Carol. Rookie biography.
E457.905.G74   1989
973.7'092—dc20
[B]
[92]   89-33845
                                                CIP
                                                AC

Abraham Lincoln
was a real person.
He was born
February 12, 1809.
He died April 15, 1865.
Lincoln was the
sixteenth president
of the United States.
This is his story.

TABLE OF CONTENTS

Abraham Lincoln was born (above) in a log cabin in Kentucky.

Chapter 1

Hard Times

Cold, wet fog crept
through the forest.
Abraham Lincoln shivered.
He was seven years old.
His family was moving
from Kentucky to Indiana.

When Abraham was small,
he planted pumpkin seeds.
A flood washed them away.
That was hard.

When he was older,
he fell into a creek.
He almost drowned.
That was hard too.

But this trip was
hardest of all.
They had to go 100 miles.

On they went—
Abraham and his father, Tom,
his mother, Nancy,
and his big sister, Sarah.
Two horses carried
all they owned.

Thomas Lincoln

At last they got
to their land in Indiana.
But they had no house.
So Tom Lincoln built
a shed of logs and branches.

It had only three walls.
A huge fire roared
in the opening.
The Lincolns lived there
from December to February.

Folks said Abraham was
"a tall spider of a boy."
He didn't like to hunt.
He hated killing things.
But he didn't mind
hard work.

He helped his father
clear the land
and plant.
They built a log cabin, too.

Abraham Lincoln helped his father build a log cabin.

Young Lincoln
visits his
mother's grave.

Then, when he was nine,
Abraham's mother died.
Sarah tried to take her place.
But she was only eleven.
That was a terrible year.

At last Tom Lincoln married Sarah Johnston, a widow with three children. Sarah was a happy person. She made the cabin a home again.

Sarah Johnston Lincoln (left) was called Sally by her family.

She loved all the children and helped them go to school sometimes. Abraham called her "my angel mother."

A copy of the notebook Lincoln kept when he was seventeen years old.

Mary reciting her Lesson.

Mary had learned to read and spell from the "Pictorial Primer" well. Could sew and knit a little too, and many other things could do, while her mother ever kind, would study to improve her mind, and in hymns of praise and love taught her to lift her heart above.

Students of all ages went to one-room schoolhouses. They learned to read from books like the American Pictorial Primer (left) and the Bible.

His school was a "blab school."
All the children studied
out loud at the same time.
Abraham couldn't go often.
But he loved school.
Most of all, he loved reading.

At home he worked hard.
He chopped trees,
split wood for fences,
and plowed the land.

But when he could,
he borrowed books
and read.
That never seemed hard.

Abe worked as a rail-splitter, cutting logs into fence
rails, and as a boatman on a Mississippi River flatboat.

Chapter 2

Many Jobs

As Abraham got older,
he kept on reading.
He kept on growing, too.
He ended up
six feet four inches tall.

When he was 21,
his family moved to Illinois.
But Abraham didn't stay
on the new farm for long.
It was time
to begin his own life.

First he worked in a store
in New Salem, Illinois.
Folks liked him.
They thought he was smart.
But he wanted to know more,
So he kept on reading.

When he was 23,
Lincoln ran for the
Illinois state legislature.
He lost.
He started his own store.
It failed.

Next, he got a chance
to be a surveyor.
He didn't know how
to survey.
So he read books
and learned how.

Lincoln's bookcase was always full.

Left: Lincoln's law office in Springfield, Illinois. As a young lawyer, Lincoln traveled on horseback going from one Illinois court to another.

In 1834, he ran for the
state legislature again.
This time he won.
But he needed a job, too.

He got some more books
and read and studied.
Three years later,
he became a lawyer.

Now Lincoln lived
in Springfield, Illinois.
He met Mary Todd
and they fell in love.
But her family thought
he was too "rough."

Abraham and Mary
waited almost three years.
Then, in 1842,
they were married.

19

Abraham Lincoln made this toy wagon for his son Tad.

Soon Robert was born.
The Lincolns bought a house.
They had three more boys—
Eddie, Willie, and Tad.

The Lincoln home in Springfield, Illinois

In 1846, Lincoln was elected
to the United States
House of Representatives.
And off he went
to Washington, D.C.

21

Lincoln hated slavery. He did not want
the new territories to have slaves.

Chapter 3

Slavery

When Lincoln went
to Washington, D.C.,
people in the South
still owned slaves.
People in the North did not.

Lincoln hated slavery.
He said new states
in the West
must not allow it.
He hoped that someday
it would stop everywhere.

But after two years,
he got tired of politics.
He went home to Springfield
to be a lawyer again.

Then, in 1850,
his little boy Eddie died.
Lincoln felt so bad
that he worked
all the time.

Four years passed.
Then a new law said the
western states could choose
slavery if they wanted.

An 1858 photograph
of Abraham Lincoln

People gathered in front of Lincoln's home in Springfield to hear him speak. Lincoln is the tall man in white standing at the right of the doorway.

That made Lincoln angry.
He gave speeches.
He said slavery was a "cancer."
It went against the
Declaration of Independence.

Stephen Douglas (1813-1861) was called "The Little Giant." Abraham Lincoln was called "Old Abe."

In 1858, he ran for the U.S. Senate. Stephen Douglas ran, too.

Douglas was a little man with a big voice. He said each state should decide about slavery. He said the Constitution was only for white people.

Lincoln and Douglas held seven debates. Thousands of people came. Lincoln lost the election. But he said, "The fight must go on."

NOIS BORN UNDER THE ORDINANCE OF '87

"WESTWARD THE STAR OF EMPIRE TAKES ITS WAY:
THE GIRLS LINK ON TO LINCOLN.
THEIR MOTHERS WERE FOR CLAY."

ABE
THE
GIANT-KILLER

THE
LITTLE GIANT
CHAWING UP
OLD ABE

BEALE P.I.

The Republican convention met in Chicago, Illinois.

Then, in 1860,
the Republicans chose Lincoln
to run for president.
He won!

States in the South
were not happy about that.
They decided to form
their own nation.

Soon eleven states
left the Union.
On April 12, 1861,
the Civil War began.

President Abraham Lincoln and Vice President Hannibal Hamlin

President Lincoln (center) met with Allan Pinkerton (left) and General John A. McClellan at Antietam in 1862.

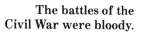

The battles of the Civil War were bloody.

Chapter 4

War

"The war won't last long,"
many people said.
"The North has more
factories and soldiers."

But the South
had better generals.
They kept winning battles.
President Lincoln was
worried.

An 1861 portrait
of Abraham Lincoln

His only happy times
were with his family.
Then, in 1862,
his son Willie died.

"It is hard, hard
to have him die!"
said Lincoln.

Willie (left) died in 1862.

The Lincoln family portrait, painted in 1861,
from left to right, Mary, Willie,
Robert (standing), Tad, and Abraham

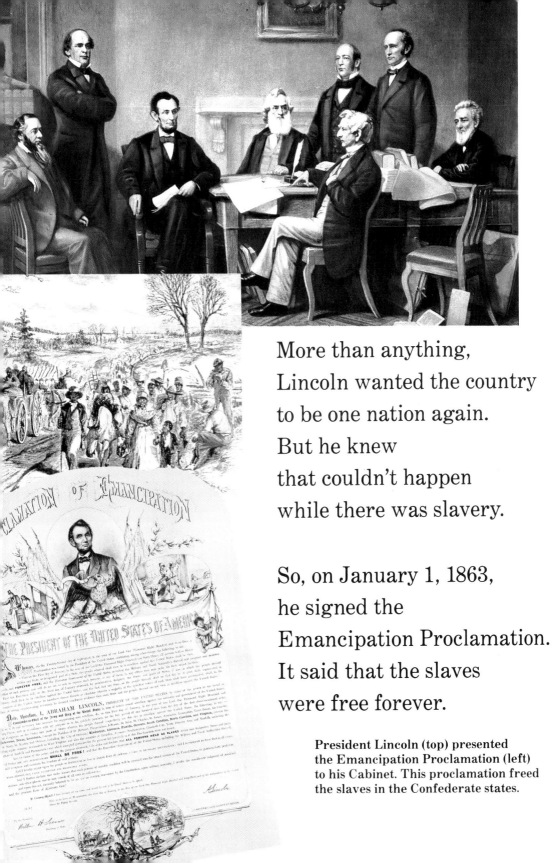

More than anything,
Lincoln wanted the country
to be one nation again.
But he knew
that couldn't happen
while there was slavery.

So, on January 1, 1863,
he signed the
Emancipation Proclamation.
It said that the slaves
were free forever.

President Lincoln (top) presented the Emancipation Proclamation (left) to his Cabinet. This proclamation freed the slaves in the Confederate states.

The Battle of Gettysburg was fought from July 1 to July 3, 1863.

But the war went on.
The worst battle was
at Gettysburg, Pennsylvania.
The North won.
But over 50,000 soldiers died.

Lincoln gave a speech there.
He said the war must prove
that America's government
could work.
It was a short speech,
but a great one.

President Lincoln spoke at the dedication of the
Gettysburg National Cemetery on November 19, 1863.

More than 600,000 soldiers died during the Civil War.

At last the North
won more battles.
But thousands and thousands
of soldiers still died.
Lincoln said his heart
felt heavy as lead.

He didn't think
people would elect him
president again.
But by November 1864,
everyone saw that the North
would win the war.

So they reelected Abraham Lincoln.

The 1865 inauguration of Abraham Lincoln (above) was followed by a reception at the White House.

Most of the Civil War battles took place in the South. After the war,
many cities such as Richmond (above) were in ruins. Lincoln,
shown below with his son Tad, wanted the North to help the South rebuild.

Chapter 5

To the Ages

After four years of fighting
the Civil War ended.
Over 600,000 people died.
Cities and farms lay in ruins.

"Now people must help
one another," said Lincoln.
He didn't hate the South.
He knew North and South
must be one nation again.

This photograph of Abraham Lincoln was taken on April 9, 1865.

But some people hated Lincoln.
They wrote him ugly letters.
They said they
would kill him.
Lincoln's friends worried.

The Lincolns sat in a private box at Ford's Theatre (above left).

On April 14, 1865,
Abraham and Mary
went to Ford's Theatre.
They sat with friends.
A guard stood
outside their box.

But after a while,
the guard left his post.
A man called
John Wilkes Booth
came into the box.
He shot President Lincoln.

Then Booth jumped
down to the stage.
He broke his leg.
But he got away.
Later he was killed
in a barn in Virginia.

Soldiers took Lincoln
to a nearby house.
Five doctors worked
on him all night.
But they couldn't save him.

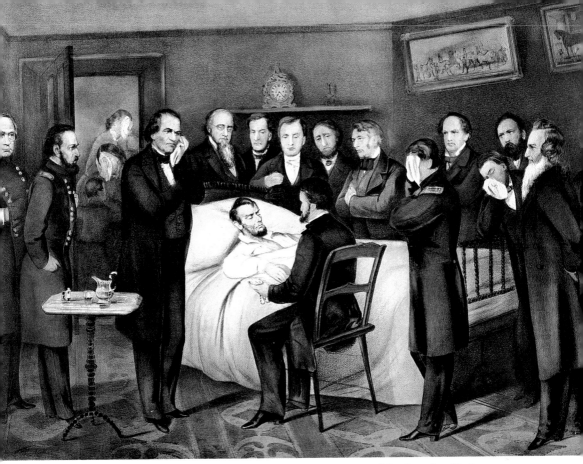

Abraham Lincoln was fifty-six years old when he died.

Early on April 15,
Abraham Lincoln died.
He was 56 years old.

"Now he belongs
to the ages,"
said his friend
Edwin Stanton.

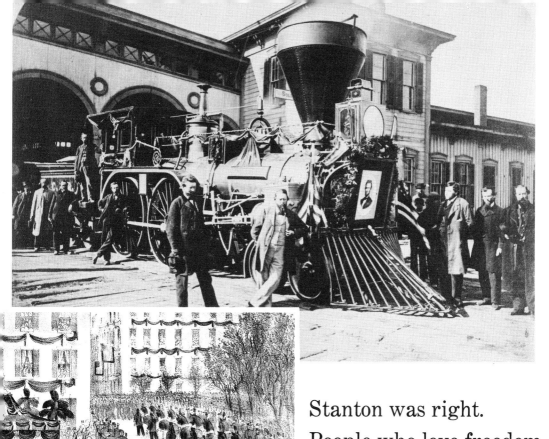

Stanton was right.
People who love freedom
can never forget
Abraham Lincoln.

Lincoln's body was carried by
train from Washington, D.C., to
Springfield, Illinois. Funeral
processions were held in big
cities such as New York so that
people could say good-bye to
Lincoln. More than one hundred
years later people still honor
Lincoln by visiting the Lincoln
Memorial in Washington, D.C.

Important Dates

1809 February 12—Born near Hodgenville, Kentucky, to Tom and Nancy Lincoln

1816 Moved to Indiana

1830 Moved to Illinois

1834 Elected to Illinois state legislature

1842 Married Mary Todd

1846 Elected to United States House of Representatives

1858 Debated with Stephen Douglas

1860 Elected president of the United States

1863 Signed Emancipation Proclamation
Gave Gettysburg Address

1864 Reelected president

1865 April 15—Died in Washington, D.C.

INDEX

Page numbers in boldface type indicate illustrations.

PICTURE ACKNOWLEDGMENTS

Cover, Steve Dobson; 2, Historical Pictures Service, Chicago; 4, (top) James Rowan, (bottom) Historical Pictures Service, Chicago; 7, Abraham Lincoln Museum, Harrogate, Tennessee; 8, James Rowan; 9, The Granger Collection, New York; 10, (top) The Granger Collection, New York, (bottom) Northwind Picture Archive; 11, (2 photos) The Granger Collection, New York; 12, The Granger Collection, New York; 13, The Granger Collection, New York; 14, (2 photos) Historical Pictures Service, Chicago; 16, Historical Pictures Service, Chicago; 17, Northwind Picture Archive; 18, (left) James Rowan, (right) Historical Pictures Service, Chicago; 19, (2 photos) Library of Congress; 20, The Granger Collection, New York; 21, James Rowan; 22, The Granger Collection, New York; 24, The Library of Congress; 25, The Library of Congress; 26, The Granger Collection, New York; 27, The Granger Collection, New York; 28, The Granger Collection, New York; 29, Historical Pictures Service, Chicago; 30, (3 photos) Historical Pictures Service, Chicago; 31, Northwind Picture Archive; 32, (top) Historical Pictures Service, Chicago, (bottom) The Granger Collection, New York; 33, (top) The Granger Collection, New York, (middle) Historical Pictures Service, Chicago, (bottom) Library of Congress; 34, The Granger Collection, New York; 35, The Granger Collection, New York; 36, The Granger Collection, New York; 37, (top) Historical Pictures Service, Chicago, (bottom) The Granger Collection, New York; 38, (2 photos) The Granger Collection, New York; 40, Library of Congress; 41, (top) Historical Pictures Service, Chicago, (bottom) Northwind Picture Archive; 42, The Granger Collection, New York; 43, The Granger Collection, New York; 44, The Granger Collection, New York; 45, (top) Library of Congress, (middle) The Granger Collection, New York, (bottom) Photri

ABOUT THE AUTHOR

Carol Greene has degrees in English Literature and Musicology. She has worked in international exchange programs, as an editor, and as a teacher. She now lives in St. Louis, Missouri, and writes full-time. She has published more than seventy books. Others in the Rookie Biographies series include *Benjamin Franklin, Pocahontas, Martin Luther King, Jr., Christopher Columbus, Robert E. Lee,* and *Ludwig van Beethoven.*